GW01182569

Leap Year
Torn Apart

The creations in this volume belong to

"Memoria Cordis media"

c/o Alex Khayutin, Hamilton, Canada
Copyright © by Alex Khayutin All rights reserved.
Canadian International Standard Book Number
(ISBN):
978-1-0688661-4-2

Dedication

*To my daughter, **Sarah**, whose mere presence inspired these lines as she grew up; and to **Netta**, **David**, and **Daniel**, who continue their grandmother's legacy with love and pride.*

***

The rhymed tale "Leap Year Torn Apart" was born out of my expression of emotions and thoughts about my mother Sarah Fradis' tragic passing during Stalinist times in Russia due to her commitment to her Jewish faith.

I wanted to share and highlight her courage, determination, and the sacrifices she made for her beliefs.

My mother's legacy has left a deep impact on me. I often reflect on how her commitment to her faith, even in the face of adversity, connects to important life decisions.

In many respects her legacy has shaped our family's values and beliefs. I am convinced it can continue doing so for future generations. The strength and resilience she showed in holding on to her identity during challenging times continues to inspire me and our family's choices.

When it comes to family and passing down of traditions, different religions share many common values. One of the most important is how children help preserve and honor family legacies and beliefs.

That is why my children' and their spouses' choices and decisions in this regard are so very important to me, especially in how these choices could contribute to preserving and honoring my mother's legacy.

I hope that my children's choices will reflect the deep significance of family, given the history and values I share in this tale. I also hope the tale will impact their future choices, just as my mother's legacy continues to impact me and them.

With love to Joe, Alysha and Leeann, who made my children happy, and to Sarah, Netta, David and Daniel, who continue inspiring me.

Alex Khayutin

"LEAP YEAR TORN APART

OR WHAT MY MOTHER NEVER TOLD ME ABOUT
ORPHAN TEARS"

A Rhymed Tale

Translated from Russian

English Elegiac Interpretation and Editing

by Jayne Berland

1982

We've dispersed, gone away,
Amid luggage of feelings, oddities, passions,
Half clad in insults like any Jew,
Half battered like one.

Without hesitation or bragging,
About going to build "the Third Temple",
We just left, carrying only children,
Two-three suitcases,
And no past regrets.

Yes, no regrets!
But forgetting? - Hardly ever!
Forgiving "them" our every tear?
Why?

Because despite everything
They'd let us out?
Out, with children, alive,
Instead of jail.

Ours are years of torrent,
Years of Jewish outpouring
Of a stream to freedom,
With no end and no boundaries.

***

For everyone, an ancient noisy Nevsky*
Is turning under the angle of its own,
I leave tears behind,
Going boldly back in time,

To witness that old train station,
Myself holding grandma's hand,
And that green separating set of lights,
Tearing our family so firmly apart,

...I am ten in nineteen hundred fifty six,
That bubbly tasting year,
When grandma and I came
To greet my arriving father,
Returning from a very lengthy
So-called "Business trip",

I could not possibly understand
How absurd was that navy-blue train,
Distant belt of iron rails
Shinny and beaming like water drop
On glass,

Or was it a tear...

Thousands of you, "former inmates"
Were coming back,
Twentieth Party Congress** still sounding
In your ears,

You, whispering: "here it is,
The new beginnings,
For which we bore
Our heavy crosses,

For which malicious scurvy
Stole our teeth
On Siberian deportation points,
While guards gobbled up food parcels,
Sent to us, forgotten in taigas".

...Grandma, walked under the station vaults,
Small package held in her hand,
Bulky, steamy locomotive crawling in,
And a small ice cream slab,
Melting in my hand,

...Ah, the childhood joy
Of an ice cream!
It was not eaten –
It was comprehended,

Little by little!
Forever wrapped into sounds
Of May Day parades,
Hidden in pressed, waffled leaves,

Torn out of the Cinderella's story,
That ice cream,
A silvery point in darkness,
Like frost, like snowflakes on a wall
Of that room,

Less than hundred square feet,
We were renting,
Where often, at minus twenty
With strong winds outside,
Teapot water froze overnight.

...Four lengthy years of living,
Wasted in Shuvalovo***,
Of weekly post office comings
To check for a sparse letter,

Of spending - cut to a minimum,
Of a band trimmed lampshade.
Of a kindergarten, leading to school,
Of a fairy tale read at bedtime,
Or, sometimes, not read,
Replaced by loud tears of punishment,

And that bulky mass of brick
At the "Lanskaya" railway station,
Bearing the strangest of names –
"Social Services Department",

Where mow eyed man
Would, at once, change
My merry and cheerful grandma
Into a cold and chilly "guardian",

Our allowance being so meager,
That once "fiver" bills were counted,
Grandma, lost and sad,
Would always evade candies and sweets,

...And here she was,
With the small wrap in her hands,
A proud Jewish woman
With the small hump on a large nose,

And even though her hands shook,
There were no visible tears in her eyes.

Oh, the salutary power of our tears,
Pushing away our grief and welcoming hopes!

...My grandma suffered insult after insult
From so many rude, ignorant men,
In silence,

"Shut up, you,
You are a mother of the enemy of people!"
They'd shout with hardly a reason,
"No - we do not know!
No - you are not allowed!
No - go away!"

...These platforms of nineteen fifty sixth,
They are like sharp fragments of memory
Inside my heart,

And that train station reunion
After four lengthy years,
Those envelopes, stamped by misery
All began in nineteen fifty two,

That leap year rolling over me,
Hurting,
Crashing...

***

1952

Today, many long years later,
That past only exists
In faded album photos,
Where my mother looks at me
From a portrait, half-turned.

A son's grief for many
Is half diluted,
A man, supposedly,
More rugged and strong,

I am, then, from a different
Breed of sons,
Not very useful to those,
Who favour such theories.

Today, I am older than
She would have been,
By four short instances –
Four years,
A fine example of how real life
Is breaking down the logic of nature,

Without a mother you are –
An eternal orphan,
Forever cursed to collecting pity,
But a goodness, born out of it,
Is of a very unusual kind,

My soul, swaddled in ribs,
Warps, pesters, groans,
And, crushing years in its thrust,
Memory is jostling me,
Back, to that April,

Of that "famous" year,

(In Russia we never had any "infamous" ones),
Each year there, marked
By a different anniversary,
When these "rank and files",
Who rose to become "higher-ups",
Would climb, in toe, onto
The Red Square Mausoleum
To observe one thing or another,

So, that year, away from the noise,
We lived in Baltiysk, which was
A small conquered Prussian city of Pilau,
Where graves of full and clean German "fraus"
Were hidden in a web of silent catacombs,

Our coziness - of a special nature,
In a spacious three-room "heaven",
With hot shower in any weather,
And a generous food allotment
Routine for a naval officer's family,

But, in this land of "joie de vivre",
Comrade Stalin could reduce anyone to a convict,
His satraps spitting equally on both,
The gold stripes and epaulettes,

Long ago, gone in centuries past,
Vile creatures began multiplying,
Today this creature has two legs,
And even a surname – Mr. Aparin.

A ranking KGBist, he smokes cigarette,
Posing a question, another question –
Writing an answer,
Question - answer,
Question – answer,
Now, verify that your answers
Were written correctly!
Sign - and zap: the statement
Becomes a denunciation!

And honestly:
It is, indeed, a "danger" to Mother-Russia,
When someone wishes to verify
The truth of the Stalin's word
Through listening the BBC!

And who?
Who?
"A rotting kike"!
An enthusiast of "freedom"
A newly aspiring "prophet",
Openly talking among friends
About defects and faults
In the corridors of the Kremlin!

With such a "bouquet of facts" –
Put the rascal in front of a firing squad!
He denies everything?
Shove pages of denunciations
Under his nose!

...So began for my father
Thundering snow drifts of Kolyma****...

But my mom, my poor defenseless mother!
How could I speak about it?
Whom could I damn?
Whose throat should I clench?

You looked at them, proudly,
Your heart slowly burning:
"Forget your husband!
Think about your son,
And yourself,
You are only thirty three!"

But how could she live,
When she was dead inside?
And whom could she trust,
When what seemed sacred,
Was reduced to ashes?

Day after day,
A week,
A month,
A second month,
The second questioning by the KGB,
The fifth, the tenth,
The twenty-fifth,

Not yet a widow,
You already resemble one,
Former friends turning away,
Scared...

...Big and boorish
I picture hugging you today,
You are so distant,
Looking at me,
As if guiltily,
Silently fingering hair ringlets.

My eyes gently wandering over you...

Oh, but every Jew has Pilate of her own...

...Washed sleeping gown,
I will never ever forget...

You wore it that morning
Which turned into never-ending night,
After you left your life and my childhood,

And there would never be enough time
To look into your eyes on that picture,
And after I expire, my daughter
Would continue gazing into your eyes...

***

Ever since then, I've been amassing hatred
Towards those, you pointed to by your death...

...God save us from meetings at train stations
Set out by graves like yours!

***

While writing this,
My life flew by,
Messed around in worldly cares,
That leap year stuck in me
Like a poisoned sting of sorrow.

And not in me alone,
As thousands grew up like me,
Our life's pages torn out by the evil,
When as five-year-olds, we were introduced
To the "Stolypin" prisoner-hauling rail-cars,
Solzhenitsyn reading to us about it
Twenty years later.

...First little while,
I called my dad – an "uncle",
He, looking at me,
Badgering to a shiver...
Dusty, lengthy terminal hall,
Multiplying crowds of people
By their sufferings,

...In my father's hands, a small unwrapped
Plastic, Chinese fan,
My mother's...my father once gifting it to her...
The only thing my grandma had saved during all these times
And brought to that train station...

Must I forgive all of this?
No way!
Never!
Because if I ever do,
I will betray my mother.

... I walk this Earth with the clogged eyes,
I have sinned and
I do not always observe the Sabbath,

"They" keep on shouting at me,
Accusing me of betraying their "ideals",
Of my exodus,
Of having corrupt ulterior motifs!

God, forgive them,
And their mercenary calculations!

For,
Everything in my fate
Including my "exodus" from Russia,
Was predetermined
After "they" killed my mother,
Leaving me no choice,

The same way the doctors
Have no choice whom to heal
And must treat everyone in need,
Once they take the Hypocrites oath.

... Thus with no hesitation or bragging,
About going to build "the Third Temple",
We left carrying only children
Two-three pieces of luggage,

But remembering, oh, so well,
What it was like for us,
There!

Notes to English translation

Nevsky* - Nevsky Prospect is the name of the main downtown street in Saint Petersburg, Russia;

Twentieth Congress** - Twenties Congress of the Soviet Communist Party in February of 1956 was marked by the famous secret speech of its leader, Nikita Khrushchev, telling for the first time about Stalin purges, his abuse of power and his cult of personality; it also brought about mass liberation of thousands of political prisoners;

Shuvalovo*** - the name of one of the suburbs of Saint Petersburg;

Kolyma***** - the name of the Russian Far Eastern region with subarctic climate, which has been known since the late 1920s as the area housing multitudes of forced labour camps, holding tens of thousands of political and other prisoners;

Russian Original

Мы разбрелись, мы разошлись по свету,
Со скарбом дум, различий и страстей,
Для всяческих обид полураздеты,
Полузабиты, как любой еврей.

Без колебаний и без манифестов,
О том, что едем строить «Третий Храм»,
А лишь детей, два-три багажных места,
И не жалеть о том, что было там.

Да, не жалеть! Но позабыть? Едва-ли!
Но «им» простить все слезы? Почему?
За то, что все-же нас повыпускали,
Живых, с детьми, сюда, а не в тюрьму?

Мы – сорок лет вселенского потопа,
Еврейского исхода сорок лет,
К свободе устремленного потока,
Которому конца и края нет.

1956

Для каждого, старинный шумный Невский
Повернут под своим прямым углом,
Я слезы оставляю на потом,
Я время поворачиваю дерзко,

Чтобы увидеть старый твой вокзал,
Себя, держащим бабушкину руку,
И семафор – зеленый, на разлуку,
Которой ты нас накрепко связал.

Мне – десять, в пятьдесят шестом году,
Тот год, как вкус крюшонной газировки.
Встречать отца я с бабушкой иду,
Который долго был в «командировке».

Где мне понять, где разобраться мне,
Какой он странный, этот синий поезд,
Идущих вдаль железных рельсов пояс
Блестит в лучах, как капля на стекле.

Вас очень много, "бывших", возвращалось,
Еще звучал в ушах Двадцатый Съезд,
И вы шептали, вот оно, начало,
Того, за что несли мы тяжкий крест.

Того, за что на ленских пересылках,
Мы отдавали зубы злой цинге,
Когда конвой «уписывал» посылки,
Что слали нам, затерянным в тайге.

Шла бабушка под сводами вокзала,
В руке держала маленький пакет,
Громада паровоза наползала,
В бумажке таял сливочный брикет.

Мороженное – детская отрада,
Ты разве елось - постигалось ты!
И звуки первомайского парада
С тобой, навечно, переплетены.

Меж вафелек, прессованных листочков
Из золушкиной сказочной страны,
Ты среди темных, серебристой точкой,
Как иней, как снежинки со стены

Той комнаты, в неполных девять метров,
Которую снимали мы тогда,
Где, если минус двадцать с сильным ветром,
За ночь смерзалась в чайнике вода.

Шувалово, четыре долгих года,
В неделю раз на почту – вдруг письмо?
Урезанность, на минимум, расходов,
И абажур, отделанный тесьмой.

Последний год до школы – с детским садом,
Со сказкой на ночь, или с ревом – без,
А на Ланской, кирпичная громада,
Под непонятным именем – «собес».

Где дядька из отдела косит глазом,
Где бабушка, веселый хлопотун,
Вдруг исчезала, превращаясь сразу,
В неласковое слово «опекун».

Где выдавалось денег так негусто,
Что сосчитав «пятерки» до одной,
Нам обходить потерянно и грустно
Конфеты приходилось стороной.

Шла бабушка, пакет в руке держала,
Еврейка, мать, с горбинкой крупный нос,
И хоть рука по-старчески дрожала,
В ее глазах не видно было слез.

О, наших слез целительная сила,
Исход печали и приход надежд!
От скольких грубиянов и невежд,
Обиды, молча, бабушка сносила.

Чуть что: «Заткнись, ты мать врага народа!»
«Не знаем!», «Не положено!», «Уйди!»
Платформы пятьдесят шестого года,
Осколки нашей памяти в груди.

Четыре года жизни эта встреча,
Конвертов, штемпелеванных тоской...
Я помню, как по мне, меня калеча,
Шел високосный, пятьдесят второй...

1952

Сегодня, через много длинных лет,
Та жизнь – в альбомах выцветшие фото,
Где на меня глядит в пол-оборота
Моей погибшей матери портрет.

Сыновье горе для других – полгоря,
Мужчины, мол, и крепче и грубей,
Я – из другой породы сыновей,
И не гожусь творцам таких теорий.

Сегодняшний, я старше той, ее,
На три коротких мига – на три года,
Так нарушает наше бытие
Законы, что придумала природа.

Без матери ты – вечный сирота,
Хоть собирай в мешок чужую жалость,
Но та, что на сиротстве замешалась,
Уже особой пробы доброта.

Спеленатая ребрами душа,
Ворочается, торкается, стонет,
И, годы на своем пути круша,
Меня к тому апрелю память гонит...

В тот славный год (мы не жили в «бесславных»,
Там, что ни год, то новый юбилей,
Когда гуськом идут на мавзолей
Те «прописные», что теперь – в «заглавных»).

Итак, в тот год, от шума в стороне,
Мы жили в прусском маленьком Пиллау,
Где, в паутинно-склепной тишине,
Могилы полных, чистоплотных фрау.

Был наш уют особенного рода,
На офицерском сытном продпайке,
В просторном и трехкомнатном «райке»,
С горячим душем в зной и непогоду.

Но, в государстве «радости и света»,
Тогда хватали скопом всех подряд,
Плюя на золотых нашивок ряд,
Равно, как на погонные просветы.

Давным-давно, затеряны в веках,
Зачем-то размножаться стали твари,
Сегодня эта тварь – на двух ногах,
И даже есть фамилия – Апарин.

Чин контрразведки курит сигарету,
Вопрос-ответ, вопрос-ответ, вопрос,
Проверьте, как записаны ответы!
И превратился протокол – в донос!

И то сказать, опасно для Руси,
Хоть отрекись от дедушки Попова,
Когда желают через Би-Би-Си
Проверить правду сталинского слова!

Сказать-бы кто? А тут – «пархатый жид»!
Свободомысл, наладился в пророки,
И при друзьях толкует про пороки,
И про кремлевской власти этажи!

С таким букетом – к стенке подлеца!
Все отрицает? В нос листки доноса!
Так начинались для моего отца
Колымские буранные заносы...

О, мамочка! Как выговорить мне?
Как проклинать? Кому вцепиться в горло?
Ты им тогда в глаза глядела гордо,
Душой горя на медленном огне.

«Забудьте мужа, думайте о сыне,
И о себе, вам только тридцать три!»
Но как-же жить, когда мертво внутри?
И верить, как, когда сожгли святыню?

Так день за днем, неделя, месяц, два,
Второй допрос, десятый, двадцать пятый,
Как-будто бы вдова, и не вдова,
Все отвернулись, кто дружил когда-то.

Я обнимаю прежнюю тебя,
Сегодняшний, большой, мужиковатый,
А ты глядишь, как будто виновато,
Волос колечки молча теребя.

Мой по тебе блуждает нежный взгляд,
Но каждому еврею – по Пилату,

Застиранный домашний твой халат,
До смерти не забыть того халата...

Ты в нем была в то утро, утро – ночь!
Когда ушла из жизни и из детства,

И мне в твои глаза не наглядеться,
А я умру, смотреть в них будет дочь.

Я ненависть с годами накопил,
На тех, кого ты смертью указала.
Не дай нам Бог, чтоб встречи на вокзалах
Вели начало от таких могил!

1982

Пока писал, полжизни пробежало,
В полувозне, среди мирских забот,
Но, как беды отравленное жало,
Торчит во мне тот високосный год.

Не я один, нам имя – миллион,
Кому судьбы повырваны страницы,
В пять лет знаком «столыпинский» вагон,
А в двадцать лет прочитан Солженицын.

Я папу долго «дядей» называл,
А он смотрел затравленно до дрожи...
Запыленный вокзальный длинный зал,
Толпу людей на их страданья множил.

В руках отца – развернутый пакет,
Пластмассовый, китайский мамин веер...

Им все простить? Навечно – нет и нет!!
Чтоб маму не предать и ...Голду Меир.

Ее отцу «всадили» в протокол,
Мол, клевета, «шпионские затеи»,
Что в синагоге целовать подол
Бросались ей московские евреи.

...Я по земле бреду закрыв глаза,
Я грешен был, и я не чту «субботу»,
Они кричат, что я уехал «за»!
Прости им Бог корыстность их расчетов!

Как доктора не могут выбирать
Кого лечить, по клятве Гиппократа,
Так за меня решилось все когда-то,
Когда «они» мою убили мать.

...Без колебаний, и без манифестов
О том, что едем строить «Третий Храм»,
А лишь детей да два багажных места,
Но мы-то знаем, КАК нам было там!

Mother

Father

Grandmother

Alik, age 7

Milton Keynes UK
Ingram Content Group UK Ltd.
UKHW021931011224
451790UK00006B/116